No Bad Parts, Only Hidden Powers

Transform Trauma into Strength

BY

Dr. Zoe Hartman

Copyright©2024 *Dr. Zoe Hartman*

All Rights Reserved

Table of Content

Introduction 8

Chapter 1 10

Redefining "Bad" Parts—Why Your Shadows Hold Strength 10

    The Myth of Brokenness 11

    Meet Your Internal Family 12

    The Protector Parts: Not Your Enemy 13

    From Shadows to Strengths 14

    The Shift Begins Now 15

Chapter 2 18

The Exiles—Unlocking the Power of Vulnerability 18

    Who Are Your Exiles? 19

    Vulnerability: The Secret Power of the Exiles 20

    Why Exiles Get Buried (and Why They Deserve to Be Rescued) 21

    How to Reconnect with Your Exiles (Without Feeling Overwhelmed) 23

    Restoring the Exiles' Trust 24

    Embracing the Power of Your Exiles 25

Chapter 3 28

The Power of Self—Becoming the Compassionate Leader of Your Inner World 28

    Who (or What) Is Your Self? 29

    Recognizing When You're in Your Self 30

    The Self as the Leader of Your Inner System 32

    Connecting with Your Self (Even When It Feels Hard) 33

    The Magic of Self-Compassion 34

    Leading Your Parts Toward Healing 35

    The Power of Leading from Your Self 36

Chapter 4 38

The Protectors—Your Inner Guardians (and How to Reprogram Them) 38

    What Are Protectors and Why Are They So Important? 39

    How Protectors Develop and What They're Trying to Achieve 41

    Understanding the Strategies of Your Protectors 41

    Communicating with Your Protectors 43

    Reprogramming Your Protectors 45

    The Benefits of a Balanced Internal Team 46

    Integrating Your Protectors into a Healthier Whole 47

Chapter 5 48

The Exiles—Healing Your Inner Wounds and Reclaiming Your Authentic Self 48

    Understanding Exiles—The Hidden Parts of You 49

    Recognizing the Influence of Your Exiles 50

    Approaching Your Exiles with Compassion 51

    Healing and Integrating Your Exiles 52

    The Benefits of Healing Your Exiles 54

Chapter 6 58

The Healing Journey—Integrating Your Inner Parts for a Balanced Life 58

    The Importance of Integration 59

    Steps to Integrate Your Inner Parts 60

    Practical Exercises for Integration 63

    Overcoming Challenges in Integration 65

    The Benefits of Integration 66

    Continuing the Journey 67

Chapter 7 68

The Shadow Self—Embracing and Healing Your Hidden Self 68

    Why Embrace Your Shadow Self? 70

    Steps to Embrace and Heal Your Shadow Self 71

    Practical Exercises for Embracing the Shadow Self 74

    Overcoming Challenges in Shadow Work 75

    The Benefits of Embracing Your Shadow Self 76

Chapter 8 78

Nutrition Myths That Are Killing You Faster 78

    The Myth of the Perfect Diet 78

    Carbs Are the Enemy 79

    All Fats Are Bad 80

    You Need to Drink Eight Glasses of Water a Day 81

    Eating Late at Night Causes Weight Gain 81

    Detox Diets Are Necessary 82

    Supplements Are a Magic Bullet 83

    Low-Fat and Fat-Free Products Are Healthier 83

    Vegetarian and Vegan Diets Are Automatically Healthy 84

    The Benefits of Debunking Nutrition Myths 85

    Tips for Navigating Nutrition Advice 86

    Continuing Your Journey to Healthy Eating 86

Chapter 9 88

Fitness That Defies Time—Building Ageless Strength................88
    The Foundation of Ageless Fitness 88
    Creating an Effective Fitness Plan...91
    Addressing Common Fitness Challenges 94
    The Benefits of Ageless Fitness...95
    Continuing Your Fitness Journey 96
Conclusion 98

Introduction

Welcome to *No Bad Parts, Only Hidden Powers: Transform Trauma into Strength*, a journey into unlocking your true potential by embracing all parts of yourself—especially the ones you've been told to hide, deny, or ignore. This isn't your typical self-help book where you're asked to "fix" yourself. Instead, we'll explore the groundbreaking concept that there are *no* bad parts within us—just parts that have been misunderstood, neglected, or hurt.

Imagine if the emotions or habits you've always struggled with—those moments of anxiety, anger, or self-doubt—weren't flaws to overcome but powerful allies waiting to help you heal. By using the Internal Family Systems (IFS) model, we'll guide you through transforming those seemingly negative aspects of your psyche into sources of strength and resilience. You'll learn how to face your trauma, release your inner critic, and welcome the full spectrum of your emotions.

In this book, we'll walk you through real-life stories, practical exercises, and powerful tools to help you make peace with the parts of yourself you've labeled "bad." We'll show you how to harness these hidden powers and use them to create a life of inner balance, confidence, and wholeness. This isn't about perfection; it's about finding harmony with every part of you—even the parts that hurt the most.

Let's dive into the transformative power of self-compassion and inner connection. Because once you stop fighting yourself, you'll realize there are no bad parts—just untapped potential.

Chapter 1

Redefining "Bad" Parts—Why Your Shadows Hold Strength

Have you ever caught yourself thinking, *"I wish I could just get rid of this part of me"*? Maybe it's the part that feels too anxious, too angry, too afraid—or the part that's never quite good enough. We all have those moments when we wish we could just "fix" ourselves. We've been taught to see our inner struggles as weaknesses, flaws, or "bad parts" of who we are. But here's a secret: those so-called "bad parts" might just be your hidden superpowers.

What if, instead of trying to silence or banish these parts, we started to listen to them? What if we could transform the parts of ourselves we've labeled as "bad" into powerful allies? This is the promise of the Internal Family Systems (IFS) approach—a life-changing way of seeing yourself that says: *There are no bad parts.*

In this chapter, we're going to explore what that really means. Spoiler alert: The parts of you that seem the most broken are actually doing everything they can to protect you. They've been misunderstood, pushed aside, or buried deep inside. But if you learn to work with them instead of against them, they'll show you their strength—and, in turn, your true power.

The Myth of Brokenness

We live in a world that loves to label things as "broken" or "flawed." From social media to self-help culture, we're constantly bombarded with messages that tell us to fix what's wrong, whether it's our mindset, our body, our career, or even our relationships. The narrative goes something like this: *"If only I could get rid of this part of myself, everything would be better."*

But here's the thing—those "broken" parts of you are actually not broken at all. They're protective. They've adapted to help you survive life's challenges. The anxious part of you? It's just trying to keep you safe. The part that gets angry? It's standing up for you in a world that can feel overwhelming. These parts may seem like they're causing chaos, but deep down, they're working hard to protect you from pain, disappointment, or fear.

In IFS, we recognize that every part of us has a purpose. There are no mistakes or flaws in our internal system—just misunderstood parts that need to be heard, respected, and integrated.

Meet Your Internal Family

IFS is based on the idea that our mind is not a single, unified entity, but rather an *internal family* made up of different parts, each with its own voice, feelings, and role. It's like having a cast of characters inside you, each playing a part in how you respond to the world.

These parts fall into different categories. First, there are the **Protectors**, the parts that keep you safe by stepping in to manage your life or avoid painful situations. Protectors can show up as inner critics, perfectionists, or even as procrastinators.

Then there are the **Exiles**, the vulnerable parts that hold the pain from past experiences—the parts that feel rejected, ashamed, or afraid. Finally, at the center of it all is your **Self**—the calm, compassionate, wise leader that can heal and guide your parts.

The magic happens when you, from your Self, can build relationships with these parts and transform their roles. Your protectors are not your enemies—they're your allies. They've been doing the best they can with the resources they have, and once they feel heard and understood, they can step back, and healing can begin.

The Protector Parts: Not Your Enemy

Let's dive a little deeper into those protector parts. You know that inner critic that always tells you you're not good enough? Or the part that makes you self-sabotage right when you're about to succeed? These are protectors—parts of you that are convinced their way is the only way to keep you safe.

Here's where things get interesting. The inner critic isn't trying to make you miserable. It's trying to protect you from failure or rejection. It thinks that by pointing out your flaws before anyone else can, it's shielding you from getting hurt. Same with the part that procrastinates—it's not lazy, it's scared of something (like failure or even success) and is trying to keep you in your comfort zone.

When you start to understand these parts as protectors, the whole dynamic shifts. Instead of battling with yourself, you begin to get curious. *"Why is this part of me so scared?" "What is it trying to protect me from?"* Suddenly, your inner critic becomes less of a bully and more like a bodyguard who's been on high alert for too long. And when you can approach these protectors with compassion and curiosity, they start to relax. They realize that you, from your Self, can handle things.

From Shadows to Strengths

As you build a relationship with these parts, something incredible happens: they start to transform. The protector that once made you anxious can become a source of strength and confidence. The part that made you angry can help you set healthy boundaries. Instead of living in a constant state of internal conflict, you begin to experience a sense of harmony—because every part of you has a role to play in your overall well-being.

Take a moment to reflect: What are the parts of yourself that you've been fighting against? What if, instead of rejecting them, you started to get curious about their motives? What would happen if you embraced them as protectors rather than obstacles?

As we move through this book, you'll learn how to connect with these parts, understand their roles, and transform them from shadows into sources of incredible strength. The parts of you that have been most challenging might just be the parts with the most power to help you heal.

The Shift Begins Now

By the end of this chapter, I hope you're starting to feel a shift—a realization that you're not broken, and you don't need to be fixed. Every part of you has value, and even the ones that cause you the most frustration are there for a reason. The journey ahead is about learning to work with these parts, not against them, so you can reclaim the power that's been hiding in plain sight.

In the next chapter, we'll explore the exiled parts of you—the ones that have been pushed down and silenced because they were too painful to face. These exiles hold the keys to deeper healing, and as you reconnect with them, you'll discover that even your most vulnerable parts are sources of incredible strength.

But for now, take a deep breath. You're not broken. You've just been carrying hidden powers all along

Chapter 2

The Exiles—Unlocking the Power of Vulnerability

Let's talk about the parts of you that you *really* don't want to deal with—the ones you've buried deep because facing them feels too overwhelming, too painful, or maybe even a little scary. We all have them: those memories, feelings, or parts of ourselves that we've tucked away in some hidden corner of our minds, hoping they'll stay quiet if we just keep them out of sight. These are your **Exiles**—the parts of you that hold your deepest wounds and vulnerability. But here's the thing: those exiled parts you've been avoiding aren't your enemy. In fact, they're the key to unlocking some of your greatest inner strength.

In this chapter, we're going to go where most self-help books fear to tread—into the heart of your Exiles. And before you panic, remember: vulnerability isn't weakness. In fact, vulnerability is a superpower. Once you learn how to gently reconnect with these parts of yourself, you'll discover that these long-forgotten pieces are actually the gateway to deeper healing, courage, and wholeness.

Who Are Your Exiles?

Think of your mind as a house. Some rooms are brightly lit and frequently visited, but others are dark and closed off. The Exiles are in those locked rooms. They are the parts of you that hold the pain, shame, rejection, and fear from past experiences—often from childhood. These Exiles were pushed aside by your protector parts because the pain they carry felt too big to handle at the time.

Maybe you experienced a moment as a child where you felt humiliated in front of others, and that moment created an Exile of deep shame. Or perhaps you were rejected in a relationship, and now an Exile within you holds the fear of abandonment. These Exiles are burdened with all the emotions you tried to avoid by suppressing them, and the protectors have been working overtime to keep them hidden.

But the thing about Exiles is, they don't just disappear. No matter how hard we try to suppress them, they're still there, and they still affect us—sometimes in ways we don't even realize. They pop up in the form of anxiety, sudden sadness, irrational fear, or even self-sabotaging behaviors. And until we start to acknowledge and heal these Exiles, they'll keep making themselves known, often in unexpected ways.

Vulnerability: The Secret Power of the Exiles

Here's where things get interesting. We've been taught that vulnerability is weakness. That showing our soft, wounded, or fearful side is dangerous because it might lead to more hurt. But what if vulnerability was actually your hidden strength?

The truth is, vulnerability is what connects us to others and, more importantly, to ourselves. It's in those raw, tender moments that real growth happens. Your Exiles, the parts of you that feel most vulnerable, are holding the emotions that have the power to transform your life—if you're willing to face them.

When you finally listen to your Exiles, something amazing happens: the pain they've been holding starts to heal. And as they heal, they reveal incredible gifts—courage, compassion, authenticity, and emotional freedom. It's in embracing these once-forgotten parts of yourself that you'll find true strength.

Why Exiles Get Buried (and Why They Deserve to Be Rescued)

Think back to a moment in your life where you felt overwhelming hurt, rejection, or fear. Maybe it was a harsh criticism from someone you trusted, or a traumatic event that left you feeling helpless. At that moment, your mind had to make a choice: how do we survive this?

Your internal protectors sprang into action, deciding that the best way to deal with the pain was to hide it. They buried the Exile—the part of you carrying that pain—deep inside, thinking it was the safest solution. And at the time, it probably was. After all, we're wired for survival, and sometimes survival means pushing down the things that hurt too much to face.

But here's the problem: over time, those Exiles become more than just hidden emotions. They start to influence how you see yourself, how you interact with others, and even how you approach life's challenges. Without realizing it, you might be living with a fear of rejection because an Exile is still carrying the pain of an old breakup. Or maybe you're constantly trying to prove your worth because an Exile holds the belief that you're not good enough, based on something that happened years ago.

These Exiles deserve to be rescued—not because they're weak, but because they're holding the keys to your emotional freedom. Healing the Exiles doesn't mean reliving your trauma; it means giving those parts of you the love, compassion, and understanding they never got when the wound was first created.

How to Reconnect with Your Exiles (Without Feeling Overwhelmed)

Okay, so now you know that your Exiles are valuable and worth reconnecting with. But how do you actually do that without getting totally overwhelmed? After all, these are the parts of you that have been carrying the hardest stuff.

The first step is to **approach them with curiosity and compassion**. Instead of thinking of your Exiles as something to fix or avoid, think of them as parts of you that just need to be heard. When an emotion like sadness, fear, or shame comes up, don't push it away—get curious. What is this feeling trying to tell you? What part of your past is it connected to?

The key is to approach these feelings from your **Self**—the calm, compassionate, wise core of who you are. Your Self is strong enough to handle whatever emotions come up. When you connect with your Exiles from this place, you're not getting lost in the emotion—you're guiding it toward healing.

Another important step is to **let your protectors know that you're in charge now**. Remember, your protectors have been working hard to keep the Exiles buried because they think it's the only way to keep you safe. But once they realize that your Self is strong enough to handle the Exiles, they can relax and step back. It's like telling the overprotective bodyguard, "I've got this."

Restoring the Exiles' Trust

One of the most powerful parts of this process is **restoring the trust of your Exiles**. Think about it: these parts of you have been buried for so long, they might not trust that it's safe to come out. They've been hidden away because they were hurt, rejected, or made to feel like they didn't belong.

Healing begins when you start to build a relationship with your Exiles, gently letting them know that they're safe now. You do this by listening to them without judgment, by allowing them to express their feelings, and by showing them compassion. Over time, these Exiles begin to trust that they won't be abandoned again.

As that trust builds, something beautiful happens: your Exiles start to release the burdens they've been carrying. They let go of the fear, shame, or sadness that's been holding them back. And as they do, they reveal their true gifts—gifts like vulnerability, authenticity, and emotional courage. These are the qualities that make you stronger, more connected, and more alive.

Embracing the Power of Your Exiles

The parts of you that you've been avoiding are not your weaknesses. They are the parts of you that have been carrying your most tender and powerful emotions, waiting for the day when you're ready to embrace them.

In reconnecting with your Exiles, you're not just healing old wounds—you're unlocking a deeper sense of wholeness, compassion, and strength. By welcoming these parts back into your internal family, you're reclaiming the parts of yourself that were never really broken—just waiting to be heard.

Remember, vulnerability is not a flaw. It's the doorway to your greatest strength. The parts of you that have been in hiding are ready to come forward and help you live a more empowered, authentic, and joyful life.

In the next chapter, we'll explore the role of your **Self**—the wise, calm, and compassionate leader that has the power to heal and guide all of your parts, including your Exiles. When you step into the role of Self, you'll discover just how capable you are of leading yourself toward lasting healing and transformation.

But for now, take a moment to honor the Exiles within you. They are not your enemies. They are your greatest allies, waiting to show you just how powerful vulnerability can be.

Chapter 3

The Power of Self—Becoming the Compassionate Leader of Your Inner World

Imagine having a calm, confident, and wise leader inside of you—a part of you that knows exactly how to handle any situation, any emotion, and any challenge. Now, picture this leader stepping up and taking charge of your life in a way that makes you feel grounded, whole, and in control. Sounds like a dream, right? Well, that inner leader is real. It's called your **Self**—and the best part is, it's been with you all along.

In this chapter, we're diving deep into the concept of the **Self**, the most powerful and transformative part of you. Your Self is the core of who you are—your truest essence. It's the calm amidst the chaos, the compassion when things get tough, and the clarity that can see through the noise of life. The beauty of the Self is that it's always there, even when you feel lost or overwhelmed. It's the part of you that can heal, guide, and lead all the other parts of you—the ones that feel anxious, angry, ashamed, or vulnerable.

So, how do you access this incredible power? Let's explore how you can step into your Self and lead with compassion, wisdom, and strength.

Who (or What) Is Your Self?

Let's get one thing straight: your Self is not just another part of you, like your inner critic or your protector. It's the **essence** of you—the calm, clear, confident center that exists beneath all the noise of your thoughts and emotions. When you're connected to your Self, you feel grounded, open, and compassionate. You see things from a broader perspective and can handle whatever comes your way without getting overwhelmed.

But here's the catch: most of the time, your Self gets overshadowed by the louder parts of your mind—those protectors that are constantly trying to manage your life, and the exiles that are stuck in their pain. It's like your Self is the captain of a ship, but the other parts have taken over the wheel, leaving you feeling like a passenger in your own life.

The goal of Internal Family Systems (IFS) is to help you **restore Self-leadership**. That means reconnecting with the part of you that is calm, compassionate, and wise, and letting it guide your life. When your Self is in charge, everything changes. You stop reacting out of fear or pain, and instead, you respond from a place of clarity and love.

Recognizing When You're in Your Self

You've probably had moments when you've felt totally connected to your Self, even if you didn't realize it at the time. Maybe it was a time when you were able to stay calm during a stressful situation, or when you felt deep compassion for someone (or yourself) even in the face of conflict. Those are glimpses of your Self in action.

So how do you know when you're in your Self? Here are some key characteristics:

- **Calm:** You feel a sense of peace, even when things around you are chaotic.

- **Compassion:** You feel empathy and understanding for others and yourself, without judgment.

- **Clarity:** You see things as they are, without getting clouded by fear or overwhelm.

- **Confidence:** You trust in your ability to handle whatever comes your way.

- **Curiosity:** You approach challenges and emotions with openness and a desire to understand, rather than avoid.

- **Creativity:** You feel free to explore new ideas and solutions without getting stuck in old patterns.

When you're in your Self, you're not reacting to life—you're responding with wisdom and compassion. It's like having an inner superhero who knows exactly what to do, no matter what comes your way.

The Self as the Leader of Your Inner System

Think of your inner world as a family (hence the name Internal Family Systems). You've got all these different parts of you—protectors, exiles, and others—all vying for attention and trying to manage things in their own way. But just like any family, there needs to be a leader who can guide everyone with love, wisdom, and authority. That's where your Self comes in.

Your Self is the natural leader of your internal family. When your Self is in charge, the other parts of you—like your anxious protector or your angry exile—don't need to take control anymore. They trust that your Self can handle things, so they can step back and relax.

But here's the thing: your protector parts don't always know that your Self is ready to lead. They've been so used to managing things on their own that they might resist letting go of control. That's why it's important to build a relationship of trust between your Self and your parts. When your parts trust that your Self is in charge, they'll feel safe enough to let go of their protective roles.

Connecting with Your Self (Even When It Feels Hard)

So how do you actually connect with your Self, especially when it feels like your protectors or exiles are running the show? It all starts with **awareness**.

The next time you're feeling overwhelmed, anxious, or stuck, pause and ask yourself: *"Who's in charge right now?"* Is it your Self, or is it one of your parts? If you're feeling a lot of fear, anger, or shame, it's probably a protector or exile that's taken over. That's okay—your job is to **gently step into your Self** and let that part know it's safe to relax.

Here's a simple practice to help you connect with your Self:

1. **Pause**: When you notice strong emotions or reactions, take a moment to pause.

2. **Breathe**: Focus on your breath for a few moments, letting it slow down and deepen.

3. **Get Curious**: Ask yourself, "What part of me is feeling this way?" Approach it with curiosity and without judgment.

4. **Invite Your Self**: Visualize your Self stepping in as the calm, compassionate leader. You might picture your Self as a wise, steady presence inside you, ready to take charge.

5. **Listen**: Let your parts know that your Self is here to guide them. Listen to what they have to say, and offer them compassion.

Over time, this practice helps you build a stronger connection to your Self. It's like strengthening a muscle—the more you practice stepping into your Self, the easier it becomes to lead your inner system with confidence and clarity.

The Magic of Self-Compassion

One of the greatest gifts of connecting with your Self is learning the art of **self-compassion**. Most of us are our own worst critics—we're quick to judge ourselves, beat ourselves up, or push away parts of us that feel too messy or complicated. But when you're in your Self, you're able to offer yourself the same compassion and kindness you'd offer a friend.

Self-compassion isn't about giving yourself a free pass or ignoring your challenges. It's about recognizing that you're human—that you're doing the best you can with the tools you have. When you lead with self-compassion, you stop fighting against yourself and start working with yourself.

Leading Your Parts Toward Healing

As you strengthen your connection to your Self, you'll notice a shift in how you relate to your parts. Instead of feeling like they're at war with each other (or with you), they'll start to trust your Self to lead. And as that trust builds, healing happens.

Your protectors will begin to relax, knowing they don't have to carry the burden of keeping you safe. Your exiles will start to feel heard and cared for, rather than ignored or suppressed. And as each part of you begins to heal, you'll experience a greater sense of harmony, balance, and wholeness.

The Power of Leading from Your Self

By now, you're probably starting to see just how powerful your Self can be. When you lead from your Self, you're no longer at the mercy of your emotions, your past, or your protective parts. Instead, you're guiding your inner world with wisdom, compassion, and confidence.

This chapter is all about stepping into your Self and reclaiming your role as the leader of your internal family. It's about recognizing that you are not your emotions, you are not your fears—you are the compassionate leader who can heal and guide every part of you.

In the next chapter, we'll explore how your **Protectors**—those parts of you that have been working overtime to keep you safe—can transform from inner critics and saboteurs into powerful allies. But for now, take a moment to connect with your Self. Breathe, be curious, and know that the leader you've been searching for has been inside you all along.

Chapter 4

The Protectors—Your Inner Guardians (and How to Reprogram Them)

Imagine your mind as a bustling city. In this city, you've got different neighborhoods, each with its own unique flavor and function. Some areas are lively and vibrant, while others are quieter and more reserved. Now, picture your **Protectors** as the dedicated security team of this city. Their job is to keep everything running smoothly and to guard against any threats that might cause trouble.

Protectors are the parts of your psyche that have stepped up to keep you safe from harm—both physical and emotional. They're the ones who've taken on the role of managing your internal world, often by creating rules, habits, or behaviors that help you cope with life's challenges. They're the reason you've developed certain patterns, like avoiding situations that trigger your anxiety or putting up walls to protect yourself from getting hurt.

But here's the thing: while Protectors are well-intentioned, they don't always get it right. Sometimes, their strategies can become outdated, overly rigid, or even counterproductive. In this chapter, we'll explore how you can understand, communicate with, and ultimately reprogram your Protectors to better serve your well-being and personal growth.

What Are Protectors and Why Are They So Important?

Protectors are like the inner bodyguards you never asked for but needed all the same. They developed their strategies based on past experiences and perceived threats, often when you were too young or too vulnerable to handle them on your own. Think of them as the internal emergency response team that sprang into action during stressful or traumatic times.

There are different types of Protectors:

- **Managers**: These parts are all about keeping things under control. They might manifest as perfectionism, workaholism, or overly strict routines. Their job is to prevent you from feeling vulnerable or getting hurt by ensuring everything is meticulously organized and handled.

- **Firefighters**: These are the parts that react in crisis situations. When things get too overwhelming, Firefighters might use distraction, avoidance, or even self-destructive behaviors to quickly put out the emotional "fire." They're more about short-term solutions and might involve behaviors like overeating, substance use, or compulsive shopping.

Protectors are crucial because they've helped you navigate through tough times. However, their methods might not always be the most effective in your current life situation. Understanding their role and motivations is the first step in guiding them toward healthier, more adaptive strategies.

How Protectors Develop and What They're Trying to Achieve

Protectors usually develop in response to unmet needs or painful experiences. Imagine a child who was often criticized for not meeting high expectations. As a result, a Manager part might form to ensure that the child's future actions are always perfect, avoiding criticism at all costs.

Or, think about someone who experienced a traumatic event and developed a Firefighter part that turns to unhealthy distractions whenever emotional pain surfaces. Protectors are essentially trying to handle the same issues that you couldn't manage at the time, using the best tools they had.

Understanding the Strategies of Your Protectors

Your Protectors have specific strategies they use to keep you safe. These strategies are often based on past experiences and can be categorized into various tactics:

- **Avoidance**: Protectors might steer you away from situations or feelings that they perceive as dangerous. This could be avoiding social situations, refusing to talk about difficult topics, or shutting down emotionally.

- **Control**: Managers, for instance, might use control to prevent vulnerability. This could manifest as overly rigid routines, perfectionism, or excessive planning to ensure nothing goes wrong.

- **Distraction**: Firefighters often employ distraction techniques. This might involve activities that temporarily take your mind off distressing emotions, such as binge-watching TV, shopping excessively, or overindulging in food.

- **Suppression**: Some Protectors might suppress or deny certain feelings or thoughts to prevent them from surfacing. This could mean pushing away memories or avoiding uncomfortable emotions.

Understanding these strategies is crucial because it helps you see how Protectors are attempting to help, even if their methods are not always effective or healthy. Recognizing these strategies can also give you insight into why you might engage in certain behaviors or reactions.

Communicating with Your Protectors

Building a healthy relationship with your Protectors starts with **effective communication**. Here's how you can approach it:

1. **Acknowledge Their Role**: Start by recognizing that your Protectors are doing their best to keep you safe. Even if their methods are outdated or problematic, their intentions are to protect you from harm.

2. **Engage in Dialogue**: Have a conversation with your Protectors. This can be done through journaling or inner dialogue. Ask

them what they're trying to protect you from and how they perceive their role in your life.

3. **Express Appreciation**: Let your Protectors know that you appreciate their efforts. Even if you don't agree with their methods, acknowledging their role can help build trust and openness.

4. **Set Boundaries**: Gently set boundaries with your Protectors. For example, if a Manager part is being overly critical, you might say, "I appreciate your desire to keep things perfect, but it's okay to let go of some control and allow for imperfection."

5. **Offer New Strategies**: Suggest alternative strategies for your Protectors to use. If a Firefighter part is turning to distraction, you might propose healthier coping mechanisms, such as mindfulness or talking to a trusted friend.

Reprogramming Your Protectors

Once you've established a dialogue with your Protectors, it's time to help them **reprogram** their strategies. Here's how:

1. **Introduce New Perspectives**: Share with your Protectors how things have changed. For example, explain that you're now more resilient and can handle situations that might have previously been overwhelming.

2. **Encourage Flexibility**: Help your Protectors understand that their rigid strategies might not be necessary anymore. Encourage them to adapt to new, healthier ways of responding to stress or emotional pain.

3. **Model Healthy Behaviors**: Show your Protectors what healthy behaviors look like. If you're working on managing anxiety without avoidance, demonstrate how you're facing it head-on with confidence.

4. **Seek Professional Support**: Sometimes, reprogramming Protectors can be complex, and working with a therapist or coach can provide additional support and guidance.

The Benefits of a Balanced Internal Team

When your Protectors are effectively reprogrammed, you'll notice a significant shift in your internal dynamics. Instead of feeling like you're constantly at odds with yourself, you'll experience a more balanced, harmonious inner world.

Your Managers will be able to relax their grip on control, allowing for more flexibility and spontaneity in your life. Your Firefighters will have healthier outlets for managing stress, reducing reliance on destructive habits. Overall, you'll feel more aligned, grounded, and capable of handling life's challenges without the overwhelming interference of outdated strategies.

Integrating Your Protectors into a Healthier Whole

The ultimate goal is to integrate your Protectors into a healthier, more balanced internal system. By acknowledging their role, communicating effectively, and reprogramming their strategies, you're fostering a supportive and adaptive internal environment.

In the next chapter, we'll explore the Exiles—the parts of you that hold deep pain and vulnerability. Understanding how to integrate and heal these parts, with the support of your Self and your reprogrammed Protectors, will lead to profound personal growth and emotional resilience.

But for now, take a moment to appreciate the efforts of your Protectors. They've been working hard to keep you safe, and with a little guidance, they can become powerful allies in your journey toward healing and wholeness.

Chapter 5

The Exiles—Healing Your Inner Wounds and Reclaiming Your Authentic Self

If you think of your mind as a house, your Exiles are like hidden rooms filled with old, forgotten furniture and dusty memories. These rooms are where you've stashed away your deepest wounds, vulnerabilities, and traumas. They're the parts of you that hold the pain and experiences you've tried to avoid or suppress.

Exiles are often the result of significant emotional pain or trauma that occurred during childhood or other vulnerable times in your life. They might hold onto the raw, unprocessed emotions that have been too overwhelming for you to handle at the time. While these parts of you have been locked away to protect you, they also hold the key to profound healing and personal growth.

In this chapter, we'll explore how to gently approach, heal, and integrate your Exiles. By doing so, you'll be able to reclaim your true self and experience greater emotional freedom and resilience.

Understanding Exiles—The Hidden Parts of You

Exiles are the parts of you that have been pushed away or hidden because they hold pain, fear, or shame. These are the emotions and memories that felt too overwhelming to process at the time they occurred. For instance:

- **A child who experienced neglect** might have an Exile that holds feelings of unworthiness and abandonment.

- **A person who was bullied** might have an Exile that carries the pain of rejection and self-doubt.

These parts of you aren't inherently bad or wrong; they simply hold the unresolved emotional experiences from your past. They are often hidden because encountering them feels too painful or uncomfortable. However, by avoiding them, you may unintentionally perpetuate their impact on your life.

Recognizing the Influence of Your Exiles

Exiles can influence your behavior, emotions, and relationships in subtle and not-so-subtle ways. When they're activated, you might experience:

- **Intense Emotional Reactions**: Sudden bursts of anger, sadness, or fear that seem disproportionate to the situation.

- **Self-Sabotaging Behaviors**: Actions that undermine your success or happiness, often as a way of avoiding or distracting from deeper pain.

- **Unresolved Patterns**: Repeated patterns in relationships or life situations that seem to stem from unresolved issues from your past.

Understanding how Exiles affect your life is the first step in healing them. By recognizing their influence, you can begin to address their needs and integrate them into your conscious awareness.

Approaching Your Exiles with Compassion

To heal your Exiles, you need to approach them with compassion and understanding. Here's how to do it:

1. **Create a Safe Space**: Before engaging with your Exiles, ensure you're in a safe, calm environment where you can explore these emotions without distractions.

2. **Acknowledge Their Presence**: Recognize that these parts of you exist and are holding onto significant emotional experiences. This acknowledgment is the first step in beginning the healing process.

3. **Gently Invite Them Out**: Use techniques like journaling, visualization, or meditative practices to invite your Exiles to share their feelings and experiences with you. Approach

this process with curiosity and openness, rather than judgment.

4. **Listen to Their Stories**: Allow your Exiles to express their pain, fears, and desires. Listen without trying to fix or change anything immediately. Just being present and empathetic can help them feel heard and validated.

5. **Offer Comfort and Reassurance**: Reassure your Exiles that they are safe now and that you are there to support them. This can involve visualizing yourself comforting your inner child or offering words of reassurance to the part that's hurting.

Healing and Integrating Your Exiles

Healing Exiles involves helping them process their pain and integrating their experiences into your present life. Here's how you can approach this:

1. **Validate Their Feelings**: Acknowledge and validate the emotions and experiences your Exiles hold. Let them know that their

feelings are legitimate and that it's okay to feel what they're feeling.

2. **Provide New Perspectives**: Help your Exiles see that their experiences do not define their worth or future. Offer them a new perspective, showing them that they are valuable and deserving of love and acceptance.

3. **Create a New Narrative**: Work on rewriting the story of their experiences in a way that supports healing and growth. This might involve reframing past events or integrating new, empowering beliefs.

4. **Incorporate Self-Care Practices**: Engage in self-care practices that nurture and support the healing of your Exiles. This might include activities that promote emotional well-being, such as creative expression, mindfulness, or connecting with supportive people.

5. **Celebrate Their Strengths**: Recognize and celebrate the strengths and resilience of your

Exiles. They've survived difficult experiences and have valuable lessons to share.

The Benefits of Healing Your Exiles

Healing your Exiles can lead to profound personal transformation. Here are some benefits you might experience:

- **Greater Emotional Freedom**: By processing and integrating your Exiles, you'll feel more liberated from past pain and trauma, leading to greater emotional freedom.

- **Improved Relationships**: As you heal and integrate these parts, you'll likely find that your relationships become more authentic and fulfilling.

- **Increased Self-Awareness**: Understanding and addressing your Exiles will enhance your self-awareness and emotional intelligence.

- **A Stronger Sense of Self**: By reclaiming and integrating these hidden parts, you'll develop a more cohesive and authentic sense of who you are.

The Journey of Integration

Integrating your Exiles is an ongoing process. It's not about completely eliminating past pain, but rather about understanding and embracing these parts of yourself. This journey involves:

- **Regular Check-Ins**: Continuously checking in with your Exiles to ensure they feel heard and supported.

- **Ongoing Compassion**: Maintaining a compassionate attitude towards yourself and your Exiles as you navigate your healing journey.

- **Adaptive Growth**: Applying the insights and lessons learned from your Exiles to foster personal growth and resilience.

In the next chapter, we'll explore how to navigate and address the conflicts between your Protectors and Exiles. By understanding these dynamics, you can further enhance your internal harmony and healing.

For now, take a moment to appreciate the courage it takes to face and heal your Exiles. This work is essential for reclaiming your true self and living a life of greater wholeness and fulfillment.

Chapter 6

The Healing Journey—Integrating Your Inner Parts for a Balanced Life

Welcome to the heart of your inner healing journey! In this chapter, we'll focus on integrating your inner parts—the Protectors and Exiles—into a cohesive, balanced self. Think of this process as reassembling a jigsaw puzzle where each piece represents a different aspect of your psyche. By fitting these pieces together, you'll create a more complete and harmonious picture of who you are.

Integration is about bringing your inner parts into alignment so they work together in a supportive, balanced way. It involves understanding and harmonizing the roles of your Protectors and Exiles to achieve greater emotional resilience and self-awareness. This chapter will guide you through the steps of integrating these parts and nurturing a more unified self.

The Importance of Integration

Integration is crucial because it helps you achieve a sense of inner coherence and emotional stability. When your inner parts are not aligned, you might experience internal conflicts, self-sabotaging behaviors, or emotional turmoil. By integrating these parts, you can create a more harmonious internal environment where:

- **Your Protectors and Exiles Work Together**: Instead of clashing or competing, these parts can collaborate to support your overall well-being.

- **You Develop a Balanced Perspective**: Integration helps you see your experiences and emotions from a more balanced and holistic perspective.

- **You Foster Personal Growth**: By understanding and harmonizing your inner parts, you can facilitate personal growth and emotional healing.

Steps to Integrate Your Inner Parts

Integrating your inner parts involves several key steps:

1. **Self-Awareness and Reflection**:
   - **Identify and Acknowledge**: Start by identifying your Protectors and Exiles. Reflect on their roles and how they influence your thoughts, emotions, and behaviors.
   - **Understand Their Dynamics**: Explore how your Protectors and Exiles interact with each other. Recognize any conflicts or misunderstandings between them.

2. **Facilitate Dialogue**:
   - **Open Communication**: Foster open communication between your Protectors and Exiles. Encourage

them to share their perspectives, concerns, and needs.

- **Create a Safe Space**: Ensure that the dialogue occurs in a safe, non-judgmental space where all parts feel heard and respected.

3. **Develop Compassion and Understanding**:

    - **Acknowledge Their Contributions**: Recognize the positive intentions of your Protectors and Exiles. Understand that each part is trying to serve a purpose, even if their methods are outdated or problematic.

    - **Offer Reassurance**: Provide reassurance to your inner parts, especially the Exiles, that they are safe and supported. This can help reduce their fears and resistance.

4. **Negotiate and Reframe**:

- **Find Common Ground**: Help your Protectors and Exiles find common ground. Explore ways they can work together to address your needs and goals.

- **Reframe Strategies**: Work with your inner parts to develop new, healthier strategies for managing emotions and challenges. Encourage flexibility and adaptability.

5. **Incorporate New Practices**:

    - **Create New Habits**: Integrate new practices that support the well-being of all your inner parts. This might include mindfulness, self-care routines, or healthy coping strategies.

    - **Maintain Regular Check-Ins**: Schedule regular check-ins with your inner parts to ensure ongoing communication and support.

Practical Exercises for Integration

Here are some practical exercises to facilitate the integration of your inner parts:

1. **Inner Dialogue Exercise**:
    - **Set the Scene**: Find a quiet place where you can focus without distractions.
    - **Invite Your Parts**: Imagine inviting your Protectors and Exiles to a meeting. Visualize them coming together and take turns listening to each other's perspectives.
    - **Facilitate Discussion**: Use open-ended questions to facilitate the discussion. For example, ask your Protectors what they need to feel more at ease and ask your Exiles what they need to heal.
2. **Journaling Exercise**:

- **Create Dialogue Prompts**: Write letters to and from your inner parts. For example, write a letter from your Exile expressing its feelings and needs, and then respond from your Self or another part.
- **Explore Insights**: Reflect on the insights gained from the dialogue and identify any patterns or areas that need further exploration.

3. **Visualization Exercise**:

 - **Visualize Integration**: Imagine a scene where your inner parts are working together harmoniously. Visualize them collaborating to achieve a common goal or supporting each other in a positive way.
 - **Reinforce Positive Feelings**: Focus on the positive emotions and benefits that come from this harmonious integration. Use this visualization to

reinforce your commitment to ongoing integration.

Overcoming Challenges in Integration

Integration can be challenging, and you might encounter obstacles along the way. Here are some common challenges and strategies for overcoming them:

- **Resistance**: Your inner parts might resist change or integration. Approach resistance with patience and empathy. Continue to provide reassurance and support while gently encouraging openness to new perspectives.

- **Conflicting Goals**: Your Protectors and Exiles might have conflicting goals or needs. Facilitate negotiations to find common ground and develop mutually supportive strategies.

- **Emotional Overwhelm**: Integrating deep-seated wounds and emotions can be emotionally overwhelming. Practice self-care and seek support from a therapist or counselor if needed.

The Benefits of Integration

Integrating your inner parts can lead to a range of benefits, including:

- **Greater Emotional Balance**: Achieve a more balanced and stable emotional state by harmonizing your inner dynamics.

- **Improved Self-Awareness**: Develop a deeper understanding of yourself and your motivations.

- **Enhanced Relationships**: Experience more authentic and fulfilling relationships by resolving internal conflicts.

- **Increased Resilience**: Build greater emotional resilience and adaptability in the face of life's challenges.

Continuing the Journey

Integration is an ongoing process that requires continual self-reflection, communication, and adaptation. As you continue to work with your inner parts, you'll find that the integration process becomes smoother and more natural.

In the next chapter, we'll explore advanced techniques for deepening your healing journey and maintaining the integration of your inner parts. These techniques will help you further enhance your emotional well-being and personal growth.

For now, celebrate the progress you've made in integrating your inner parts. This work is an important step toward achieving a more balanced, harmonious, and fulfilling life.

Chapter 7

The Shadow Self—Embracing and Healing Your Hidden Self

Imagine you're walking in a beautiful garden, surrounded by vibrant flowers and lush greenery. But lurking in the shadows, hidden behind the bushes, are parts of the garden that haven't been tended to—overgrown weeds and dark corners that haven't seen sunlight in years. This shadowy part of your garden is much like the Shadow Self in your psyche.

The Shadow Self consists of those aspects of yourself that you've relegated to the shadows—traits, emotions, and desires that you might find uncomfortable or socially unacceptable. These are the parts of you that you've pushed away or denied, often because they don't fit with your ideal self-image or societal expectations.

In this chapter, we'll shine a light on your Shadow Self, exploring how to embrace and heal these hidden parts. By doing so, you'll gain a deeper understanding of yourself and achieve a more authentic, integrated sense of self.

What is the Shadow Self?

The Shadow Self is a concept introduced by Carl Jung, representing the parts of ourselves that we keep hidden from our conscious awareness. These parts often include:

- **Unacknowledged Desires**: Traits or desires that you've repressed because they don't align with your self-image or societal norms.

- **Repressed Emotions**: Feelings that you've pushed aside because they're too painful or uncomfortable to deal with.

- **Disowned Traits**: Aspects of your personality that you've rejected or denied, often because they conflict with your ideal self-image.

The Shadow Self is not inherently negative. It encompasses the full spectrum of your human experience, including aspects of yourself that could be sources of growth and healing if properly integrated.

Why Embrace Your Shadow Self?

Embracing your Shadow Self is essential for several reasons:

- **Self-Acceptance**: Recognizing and accepting all parts of yourself, including those you've kept hidden, leads to a deeper sense of self-acceptance and personal authenticity.

- **Personal Growth**: Integrating your Shadow Self can lead to significant personal growth and self-improvement. By facing and addressing these hidden aspects, you can transform them into sources of strength and resilience.

- **Emotional Healing**: Unacknowledged emotions and desires can create internal conflicts and psychological distress. Addressing your Shadow Self helps heal these emotional wounds and promotes overall well-being.

Steps to Embrace and Heal Your Shadow Self

1. **Identify Your Shadow Aspects**:

    - **Reflect on Repressed Traits**: Think about qualities or desires you've been reluctant to acknowledge. Are there parts of yourself that you find difficult to accept or discuss?

    - **Examine Emotional Triggers**: Pay attention to what triggers strong emotional reactions in you. These triggers often point to aspects of your Shadow Self that need attention.

2. **Engage in Self-Exploration**:

    - **Journaling**: Write about your feelings, desires, and traits that you've kept hidden. Explore what these aspects represent and how they impact your life.

- o **Inner Dialogue**: Have a conversation with your Shadow Self through guided imagery or meditation. Ask it what it needs and how it can contribute positively to your life.

3. **Practice Self-Compassion**:

    - o **Acknowledge and Accept**: Accept that the Shadow Self is a part of you and that it has legitimate reasons for existing. Approach these parts with compassion and understanding.

    - o **Challenge Self-Judgment**: Confront any self-judgment or guilt associated with your Shadow Self. Understand that these aspects do not define your worth as a person.

4. **Integrate and Transform**:

- **Find the Positive**: Look for the positive aspects of your Shadow Self. For example, a repressed desire for creativity might lead to new artistic pursuits or innovative thinking.

- **Develop New Behaviors**: Create new, positive behaviors that allow you to express and integrate your Shadow Self in healthy ways. This might involve pursuing new interests or expressing previously suppressed emotions.

5. **Seek Support**:

    - **Therapy**: Working with a therapist can help you navigate the complexities of your Shadow Self and provide guidance in integrating these aspects.

    - **Support Groups**: Joining support groups or engaging in group therapy can offer additional perspectives and shared experiences in dealing with the Shadow Self.

Practical Exercises for Embracing the Shadow Self

1. **Shadow Work Journal**:
   - **Create Prompts**: Use prompts to explore your Shadow Self, such as "What qualities do I dislike in others that I might also possess?" or "What are the aspects of myself that I'm afraid to show?"
   - **Reflect and Reframe**: Reflect on your responses and consider how you might reframe these traits or desires in a more positive light.

2. **Visualization Exercise**:
   - **Meet Your Shadow**: Visualize meeting your Shadow Self as if it were a separate person. Have a conversation with it to understand its needs and perspectives.
   - **Integrate the Shadow**: Imagine incorporating the positive aspects of

your Shadow Self into your daily life. Visualize how this integration enhances your overall well-being.

3. **Creative Expression**:
   - **Artistic Exploration**: Use creative outlets such as drawing, painting, or writing to express and explore your Shadow Self. This can provide a non-verbal way to connect with and understand these hidden parts.

Overcoming Challenges in Shadow Work

Shadow work can be challenging, and you may face several obstacles:

- **Resistance**: You might encounter resistance from your inner self or fear of confronting uncomfortable truths. Approach these feelings with patience and persistence.

- **Fear of Judgment**: Fear of judgment from others or yourself can hinder the process. Focus on self-compassion and remind yourself that embracing your Shadow Self is a courageous and transformative act.

- **Overwhelm**: Confronting deep-seated issues can be overwhelming. Break the process into manageable steps and seek professional support if needed.

The Benefits of Embracing Your Shadow Self

Embracing and integrating your Shadow Self can lead to numerous benefits, including:

- **Enhanced Self-Awareness**: Gain a deeper understanding of yourself and your motivations.

- **Greater Emotional Resilience**: Develop resilience by addressing and transforming hidden fears and desires.

- **Increased Authenticity**: Experience a more authentic and fulfilling life by accepting and integrating all aspects of yourself.

- **Improved Relationships**: Foster healthier relationships by addressing internal conflicts and enhancing your emotional intelligence.

Continuing the Journey

Embracing your Shadow Self is an ongoing journey that requires continuous self-reflection, compassion, and integration. As you progress, you'll find that the process becomes more natural and that you develop a greater sense of balance and wholeness.

In the next chapter, we'll explore advanced techniques for deepening your connection with your Shadow Self and further enhancing your personal growth. These techniques will help you continue your journey toward self-acceptance and healing.

For now, celebrate the courage it takes to face and embrace your Shadow Self. This work is a vital step toward achieving a more authentic, integrated, and fulfilling life.

Chapter 8

Nutrition Myths That Are Killing You Faster

Welcome to a chapter that's going to shake up your understanding of nutrition! If you've ever been confused by the endless barrage of dietary advice—low-carb, keto, paleo, intermittent fasting, and the list goes on—you're not alone. Nutrition myths can be as baffling as they are misleading, often leading us down paths that do more harm than good.

In this chapter, we're going to debunk some of the most common and harmful nutrition myths that might be sabotaging your health and longevity. By uncovering the truth behind these myths, you'll be empowered to make informed, evidence-based decisions about your diet and overall well-being.

The Myth of the Perfect Diet

Many people believe there's a one-size-fits-all "perfect" diet that will solve all their health problems. This myth can lead to frustration and confusion as you jump from one diet trend to another.

- **The Reality**: There is no universal perfect diet. Individual needs vary based on genetics, lifestyle, health conditions, and personal preferences. What works for one person might not work for another.

- **Balanced Approach**: Focus on a balanced diet that includes a variety of nutrients from different food groups. Personalized nutrition advice from a registered dietitian can help tailor a plan that meets your unique needs.

Carbs Are the Enemy

The low-carb craze has led many to believe that carbohydrates are inherently bad and should be avoided to maintain a healthy weight and improve health.

- **The Reality**: Carbohydrates are a vital source of energy and essential nutrients.

Whole grains, fruits, and vegetables provide important vitamins, minerals, and fiber.

- **Healthy Choices**: Choose complex carbohydrates like whole grains and legumes, and limit refined carbs and sugary foods. Balance is key.

All Fats Are Bad

The idea that all fats are bad has been prevalent for decades, leading many to fear fats and avoid them altogether.

- **The Reality**: Not all fats are created equal. Healthy fats, such as those from avocados, nuts, seeds, and fish, are beneficial for heart health and overall well-being.

- **Incorporate Healthy Fats**: Include sources of healthy fats in your diet while avoiding excessive consumption of trans fats and saturated fats.

You Need to Drink Eight Glasses of Water a Day

The recommendation to drink eight glasses of water a day is a common piece of advice that many people follow blindly.

- **The Reality**: Hydration needs vary based on factors such as age, sex, physical activity, and climate. While staying hydrated is important, there's no one-size-fits-all amount.

- **Listen to Your Body**: Pay attention to your thirst and monitor the color of your urine to gauge your hydration status. Include other fluids and hydrating foods in your diet.

Eating Late at Night Causes Weight Gain

The belief that eating late at night leads to weight gain is widespread, often leading people to skip meals or eat fewer calories.

- **The Reality**: Weight gain is more about the overall quality and quantity of your diet rather than the timing of your meals. Consuming a balanced diet and managing calorie intake throughout the day is more important.

- **Healthy Timing**: Focus on the nutritional quality of your meals and snacks rather than worrying about the time of day. Eating a balanced meal before bedtime is fine, especially if it's part of your overall calorie and nutrient goals.

Detox Diets Are Necessary

Detox diets and cleanses claim to rid your body of toxins and improve health, but they often come with misleading promises.

- **The Reality**: Your body has its own natural detoxification systems, primarily the liver, kidneys, and digestive system. Most detox diets are unnecessary and can even be harmful.

- **Support Natural Detoxification**: Support your body's natural detox processes by eating a balanced diet rich in whole foods, staying hydrated, and avoiding excessive alcohol and processed foods.

Supplements Are a Magic Bullet

The idea that supplements can replace a poor diet or solve all health issues is a common misconception.

- **The Reality**: Supplements should complement, not replace, a healthy diet. Whole foods provide a range of nutrients and benefits that supplements alone cannot offer.

- **Smart Supplementation**: Use supplements as needed to fill specific gaps in your diet, but prioritize obtaining nutrients from whole foods. Consult with a healthcare provider before starting new supplements.

Low-Fat and Fat-Free Products Are Healthier

The trend towards low-fat and fat-free products has led many to believe these options are inherently healthier.

- **The Reality**: Low-fat and fat-free products often contain added sugars and artificial ingredients to improve taste. Sometimes, fat is necessary for the absorption of certain nutrients.

- **Read Labels**: Pay attention to ingredient lists and nutritional content. Opt for products with minimal added sugars and whole ingredients, and choose healthy fats when possible.

Vegetarian and Vegan Diets Are Automatically Healthy

While vegetarian and vegan diets can be very healthy, simply following these diets doesn't guarantee optimal nutrition.

- **The Reality**: Vegetarian and vegan diets require careful planning to ensure you're getting all essential nutrients, including protein, vitamin B12, iron, and omega-3 fatty acids.

- **Balanced Plant-Based Eating**: Plan your plant-based meals to include a variety of nutrient-rich foods. Consider consulting with a nutritionist to ensure your diet meets all your nutritional needs.

The Benefits of Debunking Nutrition Myths

By debunking these common nutrition myths, you'll be able to:

- **Make Informed Choices**: Understand the science behind nutrition and make choices that genuinely support your health.

- **Avoid Fad Diets**: Steer clear of trendy diets that lack scientific backing and focus on sustainable, evidence-based nutrition practices.

- **Improve Well-being**: Enhance your overall well-being by adopting a balanced, realistic approach to nutrition that suits your individual needs.

Tips for Navigating Nutrition Advice

1. **Seek Reliable Sources**: Look for information from reputable sources such as registered dietitians, healthcare providers, and scientific research.

2. **Be Skeptical of Quick Fixes**: Approach diet trends and quick fixes with skepticism. Opt for gradual, sustainable changes rather than extreme measures.

3. **Listen to Your Body**: Pay attention to how different foods and eating patterns affect your body. Personal experience can be a valuable guide in finding what works best for you.

Continuing Your Journey to Healthy Eating

With a clearer understanding of nutrition myths, you can now focus on adopting a balanced, personalized approach to your diet. In the next chapter, we'll delve into fitness strategies that support long-term health and well-being, helping you build a lifestyle that promotes vitality and longevity.

For now, celebrate your newfound knowledge and apply it to make healthier, more informed choices in your daily life. The journey to optimal health is ongoing, and debunking nutrition myths is a powerful step toward achieving a balanced, fulfilling diet.

Chapter 9

Fitness That Defies Time— Building Ageless Strength

Welcome to a chapter that's all about transforming your approach to fitness! If you've ever wondered how to stay fit, strong, and youthful as the years go by, you're in the right place. Fitness isn't just about looking good; it's about feeling great, maintaining mobility, and enjoying a high quality of life well into your later years.

In this chapter, we're going to explore how to build and maintain ageless strength through a balanced and effective fitness regimen. We'll break down the key elements of a timeless fitness routine that supports longevity and helps you stay vibrant at any age.

The Foundation of Ageless Fitness

To build fitness that defies time, you need a well-rounded approach that incorporates various types of exercise. The foundation of an ageless fitness routine includes:

1. **Strength Training**:

    o **Why It Matters**: Strength training is essential for maintaining muscle mass, bone density, and metabolic health. As we age, muscle loss and decreased bone density can become significant concerns, making resistance training crucial.

    o **How to Do It**: Include exercises that target major muscle groups, such as squats, lunges, push-ups, and rows. Use a mix of free weights, resistance bands, and bodyweight exercises to keep your routine varied and engaging.

2. **Cardiovascular Exercise**:
    - **Why It Matters**: Cardiovascular exercise is key for heart health, stamina, and overall energy levels. It also helps manage weight and improves mood through the release of endorphins.
    - **How to Do It**: Incorporate activities like walking, running, cycling, swimming, or dancing. Aim for at least 150 minutes of moderate-intensity or 75 minutes of high-intensity cardio per week.

3. **Flexibility and Mobility**:
    - **Why It Matters**: Maintaining flexibility and mobility is crucial for

preventing injuries, improving posture, and enhancing overall functionality. As we age, our joints and muscles can become stiffer, making flexibility exercises even more important.

- **How to Do It**: Include stretching, yoga, or Pilates in your routine. Focus on dynamic stretches before workouts and static stretches afterward to improve range of motion and reduce muscle tension.

4. **Balance and Stability**:

    - **Why It Matters**: Balance and stability exercises help prevent falls and improve coordination, which is especially important as we age. These exercises also engage core muscles and support overall functional fitness.

    - **How to Do It**: Incorporate exercises like single-leg stands, stability ball work, and balance drills. Practices like

Tai Chi can also be beneficial for improving balance and coordination.

Creating an Effective Fitness Plan

An effective fitness plan should be personalized, progressive, and enjoyable. Here's how to create one that works for you:

1. **Set Clear Goals**:

    o **Identify Your Objectives**: Whether your goals are to build muscle, improve cardiovascular health, or increase flexibility, clearly define what you want to achieve.

    o **Create SMART Goals**: Make your goals Specific, Measurable, Achievable, Relevant, and Time-bound. For example, "I want to increase my squat strength by 20 pounds in three months" is a SMART goal.

2. **Design a Balanced Routine**:

- **Mix It Up**: Combine different types of exercises to ensure a well-rounded routine. For example, alternate between strength training and cardio workouts throughout the week.
- **Schedule Wisely**: Plan your workouts around your daily routine and make time for rest and recovery. Consistency is key, so find a schedule that fits your lifestyle and stick to it.

3. **Progress Gradually**:
    - **Increase Intensity**: Gradually increase the intensity, duration, and frequency of your workouts to continue making progress. Avoid jumping into overly strenuous workouts that could lead to injury.
    - **Track Your Progress**: Use a journal, app, or fitness tracker to monitor your progress and make adjustments as needed. Celebrate milestones and

adjust your plan based on your results.

4. **Stay Motivated**:

    o **Find What You Enjoy**: Choose activities that you find enjoyable and engaging. The more fun your workouts are, the more likely you are to stick with them.

    o **Mix It Up**: Keep your routine varied to prevent boredom and challenge different muscle groups. Try new classes, sports, or activities to keep things fresh.

Addressing Common Fitness Challenges

Fitness at any age comes with its own set of challenges. Here's how to overcome common obstacles:

1. **Time Constraints**:

    o **Solution**: Prioritize short, high-intensity workouts if time is limited.

Even 20-30 minutes of exercise can be highly effective.

- **Tip**: Incorporate physical activity into your daily routine, such as taking the stairs instead of the elevator or walking during breaks.

2. **Injury or Pain**:
    - **Solution**: Modify exercises to accommodate any injuries or pain. Focus on low-impact activities and consult a healthcare professional if needed.
    - **Tip**: Listen to your body and avoid pushing through pain. Proper warm-up and cool-down routines can help prevent injuries.

3. **Lack of Motivation**:
    - **Solution**: Set small, achievable goals and find a workout buddy to stay accountable. Join fitness classes or groups to stay motivated and engaged.

- **Tip**: Reward yourself for reaching milestones and keep your workouts enjoyable to maintain enthusiasm.

The Benefits of Ageless Fitness

Adopting a fitness routine that supports longevity offers numerous benefits, including:

- **Improved Physical Health**: Maintain muscle mass, bone density, and cardiovascular health as you age.

- **Enhanced Mental Well-being**: Experience reduced stress, improved mood, and enhanced cognitive function through regular exercise.

- **Increased Energy and Vitality**: Boost your overall energy levels and vitality, allowing you to enjoy life to the fullest.

- **Better Functional Fitness**: Enhance your ability to perform daily activities with ease and reduce the risk of falls and injuries.

Continuing Your Fitness Journey

Building ageless strength is an ongoing journey that requires dedication, adaptability, and a positive mindset. As you progress, continue to adjust your fitness plan to meet your evolving needs and goals. In the next chapter, we'll explore the powerful connection between mental resilience and physical health, providing strategies to cultivate a strong, resilient mindset that complements your fitness efforts.

For now, celebrate your commitment to fitness and the positive impact it has on your health and well-being. Embrace the journey of building ageless strength and enjoy the benefits of a vibrant, active lifestyle.

Conclusion

As we reach the end of *No Bad Parts, Only Hidden Powers: Transform Trauma into Strength*, take a moment to reflect on the journey we've shared. By now, you've uncovered the truth: that every part of you—even the ones you used to fear, ignore, or silence—holds incredible wisdom and strength. The parts you once thought were your enemies are actually your greatest teachers.

Through the Internal Family Systems (IFS) approach, you've learned to stop seeing yourself as broken or in need of fixing. Instead, you've welcomed all parts of yourself with compassion, curiosity, and courage. The powerful exercises and stories throughout this book have shown you how to transform trauma into resilience, fear into growth, and self-doubt into self-empowerment.

This is just the beginning. Healing is a continuous journey, and you now have the tools to navigate it with grace. Each time a new part of yourself surfaces, instead of resisting, you'll lean in with openness, knowing that healing comes not from fighting yourself, but from embracing all that you are.

Remember: there are no bad parts, only hidden powers waiting to be discovered. Now, go out and live your life fully, knowing that you are whole just as you are, and every part of you deserves to be heard, healed, and celebrated.

Made in the USA
Monee, IL
30 March 2025

14880818R00056